Look Inside a Monster Truck

How It Works

Percy Leed

Lerner Publications ◆ Minneapolis

Lerner Publications Company
An imprint of Lerner Publishing Group, Inc.
241 First Avenue North
Minneapolis, MN 55401 USA

For reading levels and more information, look up this title at www.lernerbooks.com.

Main body text set in Billy Infant Regular. Typeface provided by SparkType.

Library of Congress Cataloging-in-Publication Data

Names: Leed, Percy, 1968- author.
Title: Look inside a monster truck : how it works / Percy Leed.
Description: Minneapolis : Lerner Publications, [2024] | Series: Lightning bolt books. Under the hood | Includes bibliographical references and index. | Audience: Ages 6-9 | Audience: Grades 2-3 | Summary: "Monster trucks bounce and ride on giant tires. How do these giant vehicles make such big jumps? Readers will get a thrilling inside look at how monster trucks work"— Provided by publisher.
Identifiers: LCCN 2023016102 (print) | LCCN 2023016103 (ebook) | ISBN 9798765608487 (library binding) | ISBN 9798765624401 (paperback) | ISBN 9798765615782 (epub)
Subjects: LCSH: Monster trucks—Juvenile literature. | BISAC: JUVENILE NONFICTION / Transportation / Cars & Trucks
Classification: LCC TL230.15 .L4434 2024 (print) | LCC TL230.15 (ebook) | DDC 629.223/2—dc23/eng/20230405

LC record available at https://lccn.loc.gov/2023016102
LC ebook record available at https://lccn.loc.gov/2023016103

Manufactured in the United States of America
1-1009614-51502-6/14/2023

Table of Contents

What is a Monster Truck?

A driver climbs into a monster truck cockpit. The driver puts on a helmet and straps on safety harnesses. With a pull of the starter switch, the engine roars to life.

Monster trucks racing

Most trucks are made to stay on the ground. But monster trucks are built to leap and bounce. They race around tracks against other monster trucks.

Monster Trucks Then and Now

The first monster trucks were made from heavy pickup trucks. People added huge tires and put bigger, stronger springs on the wheels to help the trucks bounce.

Monster trucks are made of parts that are strong and light. Being light helps them go fast and soar!

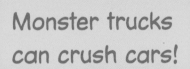

Monster trucks can crush cars!

A monster truck
with a red frame

A monster truck frame
supports the body and
the engine. The frame is
made of light metal tubes. The
driver wears safety harnesses
for protection.

People drive monster trucks in races or freestyle events. People sometimes use monster trucks to rescue people in floods. The trucks' big tires let them drive in high water.

A monster truck helps rescue people in a flood in 2017.

Built to Race

A monster truck's engine turns fuel into power that makes it go. Pistons move up and down. When a piston goes up, a spark lights the fuel. The fuel explodes and pushes the piston down.

Monster trucks have big engines!

The pistons are connected to a crankshaft. The crankshaft turns when the pistons go up and down. The crankshaft makes the monster truck's wheels turn.

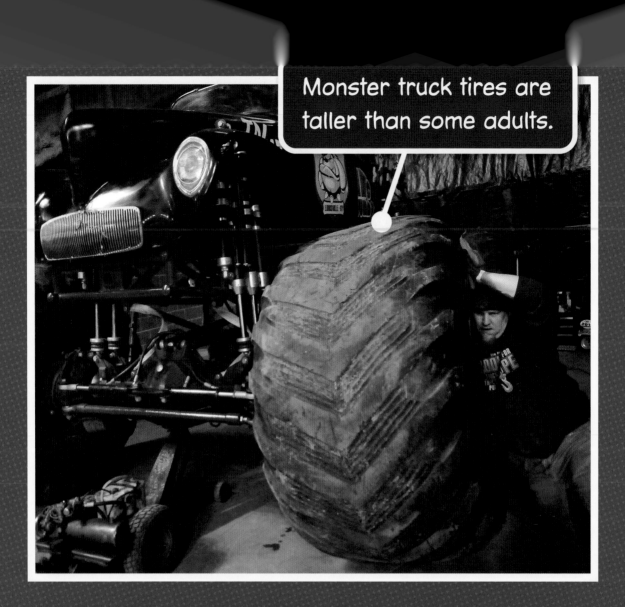

Monster truck tires are taller than some adults.

Monster trucks can plow through deep mud with their big tires. Most monster truck tires are 66 inches (168 cm) tall.

The driver turns the steering wheel to make the front wheels move. They flick a switch to turn the back wheels.

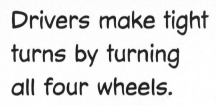

Drivers make tight turns by turning all four wheels.

A monster truck's tires are not fully pumped with air. Soft tires are less likely to burst on a big landing.

A monster truck bouncing on its big tires

Monster trucks can drive over big obstacles like other cars!

The tires have bumps on them called treads. These treads help a monster truck race over loose dirt and big obstacles.

Monster truck tires are heavy. A bit of each tire is shaved off before a race. This helps the monster truck weigh less.

Monster truck tires close up

Built to Bounce

When a monster truck hits a big bump, the ground pushes the wheels up. Then gravity pulls the wheels down. This causes a bouncy ride.

The springs are attached to the wheels.

Springs and shock absorbers keep the monster truck's frame from bouncing too much. The springs move up and down as the wheels bounce. The springs move instead of the rest of the truck.

Whether racing over obstacles, flipping over jumps, or crushing other cars, monster trucks rule the racetrack.

A monster truck competing in a freestyle competition

Monster Truck Diagram

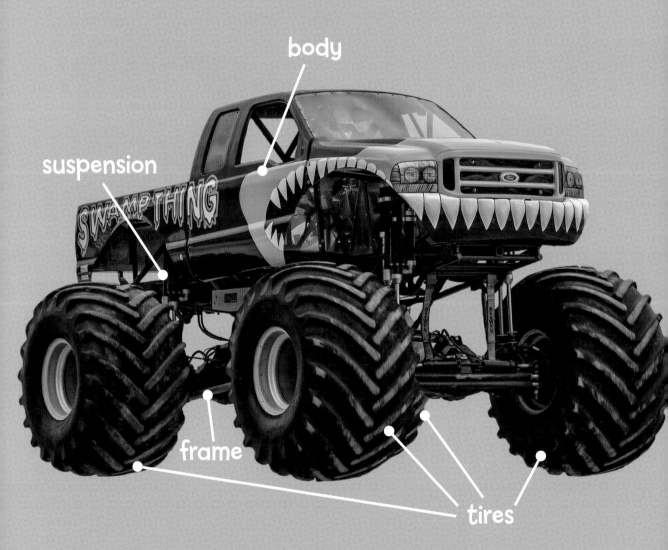

body

suspension

SWAMP THING

frame

tires

Shock Absorbers

Shock absorbers slow the bouncing springs. A shock absorber looks like a bike tire pump. It is filled with gas. One end is attached to the truck's frame. The other end is attached to a wheel. A rod moves inside the shock absorber when the truck bounces. The rod pushes against the gas to slow the bouncing springs.

Glossary

body: the main outside part of a monster truck

engine: a machine that gives monster trucks power to move

frame: the metal parts that hold a monster truck's body and engine

freestyle: a competition where drivers perform tricks and stunts

gravity: a force that pulls objects down

obstacle: something that stands in the way of progress or achievement

piston: a part of an engine that moves up and down and makes other parts move

shock absorber: a tool connected to the wheel of a vehicle that slows bouncing springs

spring: a metal piece that can return to its shape when it is pressed or pulled

Learn More

How Monster Jam Works
https://auto.howstuffworks.com/auto-racing
/motorsports/monster-jam.htm

Kaiser, Brianna. *Look Inside a Dirt Bike: How It Works*.
Minneapolis: Lerner Publications, 2024.

Mikoley, Kate. *Monster Trucks*. New York: Gareth
Stevens, 2020.

Monster Jam: Education and Activities
https://www.monsterjam.com/en-US/education

Monster Truck Facts for Kids
https://kids.kiddle.co/Monster_truck

Rogers, Marie. *Monster Trucks*. New York: PowerKids,
2021.

Index

Photo Acknowledgments

Image credits: Michael Doolittle/Alamy, pp. 4, 5, 6, 13, 19; Michele Oenbrink/Alamy, p. 7;Edward Westmacott/Alamy, p. 8; EMILY KASK/AFP/Getty Images, p. 9; PCN Photography/Alamy, p. 10; AP Photo/Chris O'Meara, p. 11; Jim Thompson/Albuquerque Journal/ZUMA Wire/Alamy, p. 12; BW Press/Shutterstock, p. 14; Bartek Wrzesniowski/Alamy, p. 15; David Lichtneker/Alamy, p. 16; Nigel Jarvis/Shutterstock, pp. 17, 20; Franck Fotos/Alamy, p. 18.

Cover: Ian Shipley SP/Alamy.